⌘⌘⌘⌘⌘⌘⌘⌘⌘⌘⌘

Flittin' & Flyin'

⌘⌘⌘⌘⌘⌘⌘⌘⌘⌘⌘

*Poems on
death, birth & life*

JEANETTA BRITT

TWELVE STONES
▲▲▲▲▲▲▲▲▲▲▲
PUBLISHING LLC
EUFAULA ♌ALABAMA

Copyright © 2011 by Jeanetta Britt

All rights reserved. No part of this book may be reproduced or utilized in any form by any means, electronic or mechanical, including photocopying, recording, or by any information storage or retrieval system, without permission in writing from the Publisher.

Inquiries should be addressed to J. Britt
(brittbooks@msn.com)
Twelve Stones Publishing LLC
P. O. Box 921, Eufaula, AL 36072-0921
www.jbrittbooks.com

Library of Congress Control Number: 2010933804
ISBN 978-0-9712363-9-4

Printed in the United States
First Edition

Editor: Fairrene Carter Frost
Cover Design: mariondesigns.com
Front Cover Butterfly: Carolyn Foster, Painter/Sculptor
Back Cover Butterfly: Laney Gulledge, Photographer
(Clayton Record Newspaper, Clayton, AL
Mayor Rebecca Beasley, Owner)

Scriptures from *The Holy Bible*
King James Version

To . . .
My Mom and Dad
who loved chasing butterflies
and taught me to love it, too.
Jason & Britt
. . . tag--you're it . . .
I'm passing it on to you.

We know that we have passed from death unto life,
because we love the brethren.
1 John 3:14a

With God, all things are possible.
Matthew 19:26b

More Books by the Author
JEANETTA BRITT
Exciting Novels

W. O. O. F.
(Women of Overcoming Faith)
(ISBN 978-0-9712363-8-7)
EMPTY ENVELOPE
(ISBN 978-0-9712363-5-6)

the series . . .
PICKIN' GROUND
(ISBN 0-9712363-3-x)
IN DUE SEASON
(ISBN 0-9712363-4-8)
LOTTIE
(ISBN 0-9712363-6-4)

Inspiring Poetry

Flittin' & Flyin'
(ISBN 978-0-9712363-9-4)
Under the Influence--Spoken Praise
(ISBN 0-9712363-7-2)

the trilogy . . .
Poems from the Fast
(ISBN 0-9712363-0-5)
Reunion
(ISBN 0-9712363-1-3)
Third Ear
(ISBN 0-9712363-2-1)

Order your copy today . . .
Your local bookstore
-or-
www.jbrittbooks.com

CONTENTS
⌘⌘⌘⌘

Freedom Song	1
I Like The Things	2
Get Ready	3
The Seasons	4
Two Seasons	5
But One Hour	6
Face To Face	7
Deep Breathing	8
Little Bit	10
Daybreak	11
The Oil of Gladness	12
Sliding Scale	14
The Way of Blessing	16
Not One Tear	17
My Mother	18
My Daddy	19
Mamma	20
Wherever Jesus Is	21
God Has A Sense of Humor	22
Love One Another	24
Gated Churches	25
A Strange Thing Has Happened	26
They Say	28
They	30
You	32
Perfect Zero	33
Revived!	34
Church In My Bed	36
Bought And Paid For	38
God Wants You Back	40
Grab Hold!	42
The Sower	44
The Weed	46
Underground	48
Your Garden	49
The World's Greatest Performance!	50
Ask Me	51
Duty	52
The Truth	54
Shout With Me!	56
Peas In The Pot	58
Blind Spots	60
'Benzes	61
Rockin'	62

FREEDOM SONG
✿ ✿ ✿ ✿

We've got this death thing
All wrong
If we sing it as a dirge
And not a freedom song.

We die daily
That's what the Scriptures say
We die to twenty-five
On our twenty-sixth birthday.

When a new day dawns
We die to yesterday
We die to being lost
When by faith our soul is saved.

Doors open and close
As we move along life's way
Preparing for our ultimate
And final death day.

Physical death
An appointment . . . not an accident
Earth's door closes
And opens one . . . heaven sent.

Never to die again
At our precious Saviour's feet
Where Life reigns forever
And from death we're eternally free!

I LIKE THE THINGS
⌘ ⌘ ⌘ ⌘

I like the things
You used to do
When you were getting to know Me
Declaring your love was true.

We'd spend time together
Just the two of us alone
No words needed
In your heart I felt a song.

Now, you're too busy
Say you're doing it just for Me
Pressing, stressing, straining
Your love I no longer see.

But I am God Almighty
My power is tried and true
If I needed anything
I wouldn't ask you.

I died and I rose
So we could be friends
So come a little closer
And snuggle up to Me, again.

GET READY
⌘⌘⌘⌘

The trees feel it
I feel it
The changing of the times
Leaves shedding, weight dropping
Getting ready for the Divine.

Nothing stays the same
On the land or on the sea
Angels whisper gently,
"Get ready,"
To you and me.

Jesus is coming back
It's just a matter of time
To take those home
Who belong to Him
And to leave the others behind.

Be in that number
To be caught up with The King
Accept Him while there's time on earth
And in heaven
With Him we'll reign.

THE SEASONS
⌘ ⌘ ⌘ ⌘

We watered and nurtured
Like so many times before
Convinced that our efforts
Would cause our flower to soar.

But the seasons had changed
To our wonderment
And our flower no longer
Could take on nourishment.

Back to God from whence it came
We watched our flower die
But on that selfsame morn
Came a newborn baby's cry.

TWO SEASONS
⌘⌘⌘⌘

She picked fruit that wasn't ripe
Said she needed it for her appetite
God held the stem on tight
But she ripped it down with all her might.

She ate her fruit out of season
She said she had good reason
But in repentance swore,
"That fruit was bitter to the core."

God gave her fruit in season
She ate it until it was gone
"Oh, what a sweet taste in my mouth,"
She sang in her happy song.

Even though her two seasons
Were the exact same length in time
She says, "It sure makes a difference
Whether it's God's fruit, or mine."

BUT ONE HOUR
⌘ ⌘ ⌘ ⌘

If there were but one hour
It would certainly mean a lot
If all the people I have loved
Could gather in just one spot.

I'd share a hug of gratitude
Offer Christ to them again
Just in case any one of them
Needed pardon from their sin.

Settled and satisfied
We were all heaven bound
We'd smile and wait for Jesus
And that blessed trumpet sound.

FACE TO FACE
⌘⌘⌘⌘

Lord, when we see You
Face to face
We'll no longer need hope
We'll no longer need grace.

We'll no longer need faith
Ruling in our hearts
Faster than eye can twinkle
Immortality starts.

For in Your kingdom
Only Love remains
And we will be like You
In Your eternal reign.

DEEP BREATHING
⌘⌘⌘⌘

My body's uncoiling
From the knot it's been in
Shallow breathing, stomach churning
Mind taking a spin.

Slowly, I feel
Life creeping back into my bones
From the bitter, hard trial
That my body has known.

Thank you, Lord Jesus
For your mercy and grace
For letting Your light shine again
So I can see your face.

But I will never regret
What You taught me in the dark
The time You used to rivet
Your truth in my heart.

You taught me for true
I need no one but You
That your work is complete
And You will see me through.

That You're nigh unto
The brokenhearted
That You always finish
What You've started.

That You watch out for me
When my back is turned
That an inheritance is something
I don't have to earn.

Love one another
And the rest You will do
Now, I'm deep breathing
My life is in You.

LITTLE BIT
⌘⌘⌘⌘

Everything, but a little bit
Was swallowed up in grief
You held my reins by that little bit
And stirred up my belief.

All alone, far away from home
How could I face this disaster?
But knowing You
You brought me through
To find my ever after.

You heaved people into my bosom
To meet my every need
You did what it was You said You'd do
When Your promises I had received.

You plucked my mind out of panic
You settled my heart down with peace
You reminded my soul I had been here before
And each time
You'd brought sweet relief.

As the trappings of my existence
Are stripped to very few
Whenever I'm down to a little bit
My life is reborn in You.

DAYBREAK
⌘⌘⌘⌘

Day is breaking
Quiet and neat
From the hand of the Lord
It's gentle and sweet.

Like life and death
When you're in His heart
You can't tell where one ends
And the other starts.

THE OIL OF GLADNESS
⌘⌘⌘⌘

"Well, Doc," the woman said,
"I must be growing old
My digestive system's sagging
Like my body and my clothes.

What pill can you give me,"
She went on to say,
"To stir up my insides
And keep them from turning gray?

I go through all the motions
Do everything I've ever done
But I'm tired all the time
Like darkness has replaced the sun."

The aging doctor slid
His tiny glasses to his nose
"Let me take a look at you,"
And he peered down to her soul.

"You've been my patient a long time
We're growing old together
You even know my arthritis
Is able to predict the weather.

But I sense there's something more
Than you're telling me today
It sounds as if to me
More than your hair is turning gray.

They've got dye for your hair
And diets for your tummy roll
But only God can give you
The Oil of Gladness for your soul.

It starts with thanksgiving
Thanking God for what you've got
And quit looking back
At the things you have not.

Stop expecting love from others
But give your love away
And trust our Saviour's love
To keep you everyday.

Thank Him! Thank Him! Thank Him!
For every single thing
And you'll feel The Oil of Gladness
Permeate your frame.

Thankfulness is one thing
Your mind can't fake
Your insides know when it's for real
And prance to the melody it makes.

The Oil of Gladness will bathe you
And fill you through and through
And the joy of the Lord
Will shine right back at you."

"You're absolutely right, Doc,
I have been feeling blue
I want to be more thankful
But what can I do?"

"Go home and take a heaping dose
Of prayer . . . with honesty
And I guarantee you'll feel much better
By the next time you see me."

SLIDING SCALE
⌘⌘⌘⌘

Nobody talks about sin anymore
Prosperity and blessing is what we're looking for
No right, no wrong, no heaven, no hell
Everything, now, is on the sliding scale.

Even truth is relative
Everybody's got their own
Your truth, my truth
Don't mess with my comfort zone.

We stress and we strain
We twirl and we lie
Trying to hide our sin
Under an alibi.

Anything but confess it
And expose it to God's light
So He can purify it
And teach us what's right.

But sin is the only thing
For which Christ died
Not mistakes, not our issues,
Or our foolish pride.

So to be set free
And make our escape
We have to call sin what God calls it
And finally make the break.

There's nothing to fear
The penalty's been paid
So it's okay to confess our sins
So our lives can be remade.

But it's like when we were kids
Out in the school yard
The fight can't be over
Until we agree with God.

But if we only want Jesus
Just enough to skip hell
We might find our blessings
Are on the sliding scale.

THE WAY OF BLESSING
⌘⌘⌘⌘

Things can't be healed
That don't get cleaned up
No matter how we gloss them over
With religious cover-up.

Pray-mo, Praise-mo
Use the Lord's name-in-vain-mo
But nothing will change
If we do the same-o, same-o.

Love for the Lord
Begins with doing what He says
Calling sin what He calls it
And agreeing to be led.

Following His Word
Points us in the right direction
We can turn, cross over
And enter The Way of Blessing.

The Way of Blessing
Is narrow; 'tis true
God designed it that way
So only truth can fit through.

There's no room in there
For self-made devices
Lies, deceit, deception,
And other vices.

Salvation is free
Paid in full by Christ our King
But to enter The Way of Blessing
We've got to come clean.

NOT ONE TEAR
⌘⌘⌘⌘

Not one tear can change it
If you die without Jesus Christ
No prayer and no regret
Can give you eternal life.

It's a sad, sad day
If your loved ones are left to say
They know you are gone
But they wonder which way.

So get it straight on this side
Before the grave's final call
Give your life to Jesus
Surrender to Him your all.

He has promised He will take us
To the other side
And in Him, we'll find safe harbor
Eternal to abide.

MY MOTHER
⌘⌘⌘⌘

Death had to find my mother
Because she wasn't looking for him
She served her Lord
She loved her enemies
And she was intent on living her life
To the fullest
And to the end.

I wear her Christmas sweater
I remember the joy
With which she wore it
And I am convinced
Death
Is allergic
To glitter!

MY DADDY
⌘⌘⌘⌘

You showed me how to laugh and love
Told me what this world was really made of
Pointed me to our Heavenly Father above
Daddy

You held my hand across the street
Stuck by me when things weren't neat
Watched over me without making me weak
Daddy

You're what I look for
In every man
Living your faith
Lending a hand

And because of your courageous stand
Your example of love to the bitter end
I call my Heavenly Father as I hold his hand
Daddy

MAMMA
⌘ ⌘ ⌘ ⌘

It can be hard touching Mamma's stuff
When she's not there to touch it herself
Rambling around in her private drawers
Pulling her church hats down off the shelf.

But be encouraged, my friend
Your Mamma did it for her Mamma, too
It's not intended to make us cry
It's the labor of love God left us to do.

It reminds us that this life
Is just a hand's breath from death
And like Mamma, we're passing through
To prepare the children who are left.

It proves our God is King
A God who cannot lie
For no matter how much He loves us
Each one of us must die.

When the bloom falls off
And the flower, indeed, doth fade
It proves we can trust Christ Jesus
For every promise He has made.

To love us unconditionally . . .
To never leave us alone . . .
The assurance that comes in knowing
We'll meet Mamma when we get home.

WHEREVER JESUS IS
⌘⌘⌘⌘

When offered living water
The woman threw down her water pots
When Mary Magdalene accepted His love
Her street walking—stopped.

When Lazarus heard His voice
He came forth from the grave
When the centurion believed His Word
His child was saved.

Think about the temple
Where the thieves were driven out
Think about the lepers
Who were left without a spot.

Wherever Jesus is
He brings about a change
When we abandon our way
And cling wholly to His name.

Our lives will magnify Him
When our hearts He reclaims
For wherever Jesus is
Nothing stays the same.

GOD HAS A SENSE OF HUMOR
⌘⌘⌘⌘

God has a sense of humor
I see it every day
He gives some folk the gift of gab
But they have nothing to say.

He gives some of us verse
And we're too afraid to share it
But a poem can only come alive
When someone is there to hear it.

To some He gives the lyrics
And to others He gives the beat
It takes two to make the music
And the melody complete.

God knows our tendency
To blow up with pride
So He won't even let us save ourselves
We need Jesus to be our guide.

Jesus died once and for all
Our souls to regain
And He alone can give us new life
For human nature will never change.

And to each believer He gives gifts
And places us in His church
So we can help each other
Keep this world from going berserk.

But if I don't accept your gift
And you don't accept mine
Instead of doing our Saviour's will
We'll be wasting our time.

And when we try to go it alone
We'll be limited to what we can do
Until we finally get the punch line
You need me and I need you.

But if we keep on going solo
Out here on these streets
The joke will be on us
Isolation brings defeat.

God fixed it this way
He's grinning from ear to ear
We need Him *and* each other
While we're living down here.

LOVE ONE ANOTHER
⌘⌘⌘⌘

Put people above process
We have only this moment to share
Put people above structure
Love is a disciple's fare.

"Love one another,"
Our Saviour left command
No alternative strategy
Can surpass His master plan.

Should every 'i' be dotted
And every 't' be crossed
It won't amount to much
If precious souls are lost.

Order and convention
Doing the same old thing
May suit our comfort level
Our control to maintain.

But God's ways are not our ways
New Wine will old skins rupture
Will a Rushing, Mighty Wind
Fit in our committee structure?

Intellectual accuracy
Enough to dazzle and amaze
Will pale by sheer comparison
When love is set ablaze.

GATED CHURCHES
⌘⌘⌘⌘

Gated churches
What a sight to behold!
Matching gated hearts
Leaving the Gospel untold

We're in; you're out
Is the message they send
Not that Jesus Christ
Paid for all our sins

Jesus walked with all
Whether publican or sinner
He healed all their diseases
Sat down with them for dinner

He guarded--nothing
His invitation--open
Come unto Me
If your heart is broken

And though love crucified Him
In the end
He swung open heaven's gates
So we can all come in

A STRANGE THING HAS HAPPENED
⌘ ⌘ ⌘ ⌘

This world belongs to the devil
We're looking for a new heaven and a new earth
But God left the church as a lighthouse
For those He's chosen for the New Birth.

But we don't know who they are
So our hands are outstretched to all
We don't know the times or the seasons
We work winter, spring, summer, and fall.

And while we wait for Jesus
To come back and split the sky
The Lord told us to be faithful
To stand strong and occupy.

To love one another
To value every person's worth
So this world can see in His church
Just a little bit of heaven on earth.

But a strange thing has happened
In the church--and it's called sin
Instead of standing on the Solid Rock
We've let the ways of the world creep in.

We fight over power and position
We fight over money and kin
We fight over things that are passing away
We even fight over church doctrine.

The New Testament--no longer our road map
The ways of Jesus--no longer our leading
We put ourselves before others
It's like our servant's heart has quit beating.

Whatever happened to kindness,
Gentleness, and meekness and such
Sometimes we don't need the theatre
We get plenty of play-acting at church.

But Jesus is calling His church
To come back to your first love
To put aside our own agendas
And give the world His message from above.

How God wrapped Himself in flesh
And died for all our sins
Jesus finished His work to the uttermost
And with all power He rose again.

And by grace through faith in Jesus
The Holy Scriptures say
We can enter into His finished work
And be saved 'til our dying day.

For it's not by deed or duty
Or any work that we have done
But God gives a ticket to heaven
To *anyone* who believes on His Son.

This is the Good News--the Gospel
Of the love and forbearance of God
And *it* alone has the power
To break a lost sinner's heart.

And a broken heart can be converted
When we tell them the truth in His Word
And they can turn from sin and sorrow
And be covered under His mighty blood.

God left this world as His vineyard
And His church to harvest it all
And He gives to us whatever we need
To fulfill His mission's call.

To invite lost souls into the arch of safety
To triumph over sin and evil and such
And when we do--a strange thing will happen
People will get saved at church!

THEY SAY
⌘⌘⌘⌘

There's a lie in the church
And it needs to be stopped
Haven't you heard it?
It started at the top.

They say, Yes,
Jesus died for your sins
And with all power in His hands
He rose again.

But in the very next breath
They say, but that's not all you need
If you're going to stay saved
It depends upon your deeds.

Now, that's heresy
A lie to you and me
It disputes God's Word
And His sovereignty.

Do you think that Jesus
From His kingdom would come
All the way down here
And leave something undone?

Jesus came to earth
So our faith could set us free
But if we believe what *they say*
It's in bondage we will be.

For God said, Believe
On His Only Begotten Son
And He'll give us His righteousness
Each and everyone.

He'll give us His Spirit
So we can walk therein
And He promised to forgive us
When we confess our sins.

He'll give us heavenly places
And call us His friend
And His grace will give us power
Unless we let doubt creep in.

So let's get out our Bibles
And dust them all off
This lie is weakening the church
And it's confusing the lost.

We've got them thinking
That we're so grand
We fail to tell them
About the Father's faith plan.

It's no wonder
We keep up such a fuss
Instead of praising Jesus
We think it's all about us.

But our deeds can't save us
It's time for the lie to die
Fill the church with thanksgiving
And let the true Gospel multiply.

So take God at His Word
Don't listen to what *they say*
If you want to be saved from sin
Christ Jesus is the only way!

THEY
✯ ✯ ✯ ✯

They don't want you to know
That you've been forgiven
For if you ever get it straight
You could really start living.

They don't want you to believe
That you've been set free
That Jesus paid for *all* your sins
When He died upon that tree.

And when He rose again
With all power in His hands
He released every captive
Woman, boy, girl, and man.

You can come to Jesus
And accept your blessing
He's already paid the price
So it's yours for the asking.

They say, Jesus is this
They say, He's that
Trying to confuse you
And keep you locked up in their trap.

They know if you ever get it
You'd no longer need to grope
For their pills, and their alcohol,
And their dope to cope.

They can't have that
It would be bad for the economy
If you stop being needy
How can they be greedy?

They don't really care
If you moan and groan
They are not for you
This world is not your home.

But if you sell out to Jesus
Then they can't sell you out
When being wrapped up in His love
Is what your life is all about.

They want to keep you from Him
Because they know what's true—
You don't need them
They . . . need you.

YOU
⌘⌘⌘⌘

When they questioned Jesus
He didn't have time
He didn't say a mumbling word
He had you on His mind.

When He was brutalized and crucified
For sins He didn't commit
He hung there for you
He stayed 'til He finished it.

His death was not an accident
Or a cosmic mistake
He bled and died and rose again
Your sins to eradicate.

You can reject His forgiveness
And leave it on the shelf
But unless it's true He died for you
Then you've got to die for yourself.

You can listen to these philosophies
That say Jesus isn't real
And that say for your salvation
You must work to seal the deal.

Or you can accept the loving gift
Jesus bought you on that tree
So . . . why would you work for something
That's been given to you for free?

PERFECT ZERO
⌘⌘⌘⌘

Sometimes in life God cuts you back to . . .
Perfect zero
Like you would a prize rose
Trimming away the deadwood
That only He knows

Putting an end to your way
And starting you over in His
Setting your life straight
And being the answer
To all your tears

As time passes
And the years ensue
You can see . . .
Perfect zero
Had been good for you

But the trick of it is
To trust The Gardner so
You can say,
"Thank you, Lord," even at . . .
Perfect zero

REVIVED!
⌘⌘⌘⌘

We've been living off the fumes
Of our forefathers' faith
Going through the motions
Trying to get by on their grace.

Instead of giving the Lord
All our faith and our trust
And letting the Holy Spirit breathe
Afresh . . . upon us . . . aaah!

We've been asleep on the wall, y'all
Falling prey to charlatans
Who extract their filthy gain from us
Again and again.

We've let selfish ambition
Creep in with bitter strife
The church is going corporate
Instead of birthing new life.

We haven't been reading our Bibles
Like it's the very first time
And giving the Lord true worship
With a made-up mind.

We need You to renew us, Lord
In the truth of Your Word
To delight ourselves in only You
And give You the praise You deserve.

We need You to help us, Lord
To love one another again
Hearts touching hearts
No fake agendas and grins.

We can't do it on our own, Lord
But we confess; we do
That we have been wrong, Lord
And we're turning back to You.

Bring back life to Your church, Lord
That has been pronounced dead
Revive our souls and fill-up our faith
By Your Spirit to be led!

CHURCH IN MY BED
⌘⌘⌘⌘

I have church in my bed
'Most every night
I start talking to the Lord
As soon as I turn out the lights.

Sometimes on my knees
Sometimes I'm prone
But I talk to The One
Who has never left me alone.

My prayers are not pious,
Or churchy, or flip
It's like kicking it with a Good Friend
In a warm relationship.

I thank Him for being God
And He wipes away my tears
As I remember His goodness
Down through the years.

All the grace and mercy
He has shown
Despite my every deed
He has known.

He's kept His promises
Even when I broke mine
And welcomed me back home
Each and every time.

I don't need a pulpit,
Or music, or pews
I get lifted up to heaven
When I rehearse the Good News.

How Jesus came to earth
To set us free
How He died the cruel death
Meant for you and me.

And to those who believe
He gives us kinship
And nothing and no one
Can bust-up our friendship.

How can we not love
A God like this?
How can we not worship Him
With the praise of our lips?

Fellowship of the saints
We need it; it's fine
But sometimes we need
Just a little closet time.

Jesus gave His all
To make it all right
So I can have church
In my bed 'most every night!

BOUGHT AND PAID FOR
⌘ ⌘ ⌘ ⌘

Our home in God's kingdom
Has been bought and paid for
Will you take possession?
The only question on the floor.

In order to take title
We have to admit
We've fallen from God's perfection
Our sin made us separate.

We are not merely sinners
Because of our deeds
But by birth we were formed
From Adam's rebellious seed.

God in His mercy
Tallied from beginning to end
Past, present, future
He totaled up mankind's sin.

In a single act of love
More amazing than the worlds He made
His Son assumed our sin debt
And on the cross the debt was paid.

With His Son's sacrifice
The Father was well-pleased
He overpowered the grave
And handed Jesus the keys.

Triumphant! Risen Saviour!
In His healing hands He holds
The receipt of redemption
For every sin-sick soul.

Come and get what's yours
It's bought and paid for
Stand outside no longer
Jesus Christ is the open door.

GOD WANTS YOU BACK!
⌘⌘⌘⌘

God wants you back
Didn't you know?
Well, He sent me out here
Just to tell you so.

He knows you've cheated
And been untrue
But He sent me here to tell you
He still loves you.

He's been wooing you back
For a very long time
Didn't His lovingkindness
Tell you, you were on His mind?

God saw you struggling
With sin from His throne
And He knew the gap was far too wide
For you to make it home alone.

So God came for you
On a cross that was cruel
Poured out His blood and filled-up the gap
To pay your sin debt in full.

Death tried to hold Him
As Satan's final action
But Jesus overpowered the grave
And completed the transaction.

He did it all for you
You couldn't do it for yourself
He stretched out wide to touch your hand
To show you, He loves you to death!

Now, it's up to you
Nothing stands in your way
You can turn around and take God's hand
On this very day.

God wants you back
It's no con and no game
You can come back home through His blood
And be saved in Jesus' name!

GRAB HOLD!
⌘⌘⌘⌘

We used to
Hold hands
Without being asked
To do so
Ring games
Prayer circles
Friends holding hands
Skipping

But, now,
We've become so
Separate
Personal phones
Personal ipods
Personal games
Personal space
Virtual world

And the more
Personal
We've declared
Ourselves to be
The more
Impersonal
We've become
Separate

And our hands
They miss each other
And our lives
They tell the story
Of a circle broken
In our homes, in our churches
In our children, in our community
In our world

But the hand of Christ
Is still outstretched
To bring us back
Into the circle of humankind
To love God, to love each other
To live life . . . more abundantly
The way He intended
Grab hold!

THE SOWER
⌘ ⌘ ⌘ ⌘

I'm going to sow looking up
Not looking down
I'm not going to try to measure
What's coming back around.

The size of the increase
Is in God's hand
I'm going to sow just what He gives me
Into His perfect plan.

Everything I have
Came from Him, you see
Nothing I have
Belongs to me.

He gave me salvation
Perfect peace and rest
He gave me all things
Pertaining to righteousness.

He gave me His Spirit
To keep my feet on the ground
He gave me His love
To spread it all around.

He gave me His Word
Just to take me higher
So the lost can be inspired
And catch on fire.

He gave me position and
Privilege and power
Purpose, possession
And provision by the hour.

He gave me everything
I need down here
So the harvest belongs to Him
Whenever He shall appear.

And whether our crowns
Be many or few
We know, Lord Jesus
It's all because of You.

And on that blessed day
We cast our crowns before the Son
I want to hear my Master say,
"Faithful servant, well done!"

THE WEED
⌘⌘⌘⌘

I pulled a weed last night
From my flower pot
Man, you should've seen that thing
It had really grown a lot.

I had watched while it grew
First little and then big
By the time I tried to pull it out
I almost needed a rig.

I pulled and I tussled
The root on that weed was huge
It had no value in itself
But it was hogging up all the food.

It had gotten so tall
It was blocking out the sun
And the flowers I had planted there
Could almost get none.

It had gotten so wide
It was taking up all the room
And the flowers trying to grow there
Were simply unable to bloom.

But as soon as I snatched out that weed
The Good News started to race
The flowers began to spread out
And take up their rightful place.

Now, when is the last time
You took a look at your flower pot
Did you happen to see any weeds
Trying to overtake the spot?

Bitterness, strife, and envy
Unforgiveness, anger, the lot
These weeds will try to take over
In your flower pot.

But the weed, I find, most difficult
Is called--'Forgetting-you-are-loved'
That Jesus Christ has paid the price
And wrote your name above.

This root runs very deep
You can't tackle it; don't even dare
It takes the power of God's Word,
True confession and fervent prayer.

But when the weeds are all gone
Your flowers will go to town
They'll bloom and they will blossom
And spread Christ's love all around.

This is the lesson I learned
And I'll pass it on to you
When we pull our weeds daily
The True Vine will show through.

UNDERGROUND
⌘⌘⌘⌘

Good seed in good soil
Will have its way
But while it's underground
We wait for that glorious day.

The work done underground
From us, it has no needs
We can't cause the seed to grow
Only water and pull the weeds.

But the seed will spring forth
And bear after its own kind
Apples on an apple tree
Blackberries on a vine.

The Good Seed in us
Is the Word of God
And when it falls on fertile ground
It will surely do its part.

But while we wait down here
And with sin and sorrow wrestle
The treasure is underground
In our earthen vessel.

But rejoice all the more
For the Good News is true
The Lord began a good work in us
And He will see it through.

And when these earthen vessels
Crack and give way
Our eternal life in Jesus
Will spring forth on that glorious day!

YOUR GARDEN
⌘⌘⌘⌘

You can stand on the sidelines
And say that's swell
You can stand by and watch
While others do well

You can pass by and admire
Everyone else's lawn
You can wait and just wait
For your ideas to spawn

But to watch your garden grow
You've got to plant the seeds and sow

You've got to see your invisible goal
You've got to draw strength from your soul

You've got to embrace your environment
You've got to pray through the elements

You've got to use what's in your hand
You've got to make your choice and stand

You've got to deal with the weeds that grow
You've got to trust God for where to go

For whether you plant or do nothing
With it comes toil and strife
And whether bountiful or bare
Your garden is your life

THE WORLD'S GREATEST PERFORMANCE!
⌘⌘⌘⌘

If heaven were based on our performance
We would all go to hell
But God wouldn't let it be
He wanted us with Him to dwell.

God searched the world over
From beginning to end
And laid upon His Son
Our each and every sin.

The World's Greatest Performance!
God judged on that day
When Jesus hung His head and died
And took all our sins away.

God raised Him from the dead
And in love, He crowned Him King
Over heaven and over earth
And every other living thing.

Performance for us is death
Against the law we cannot compete
But the love of Christ brings us back to life
When we surrender at our Saviour's feet.

Jesus Christ is Lord
Our performance doesn't matter a bit
Our faith alone opens heaven's door
On the basis of relationship.

ASK ME
⌘⌘⌘⌘

Every now and then
People make a big deal
About our service to the Lord
And then there're times they belittle it
And refuse to get on one accord.

But nothing can compare
To what He's done for us
So anything we do
Ought not create a fuss.

So when you see me do
What I'm blessed to do
Don't think of me as special,
Or grand, or whoop-de-doo.

For in His kingdom
There's work for all to do
Something designed, tailor-made
Especially for you.

So if you wonder what I'm doing
Ask me; don't assume
I'm a ransomed, blood-bought
Child of the King
And I'm just cleaning up my room.

DUTY
✤ ✤ ✤ ✤

Do not *ever* trade duty for love
It will take the very heart out of whatever it is
You're trying to do
Do what you do in love
And love will come back to you.

Duty is loaded with debt
Obligations we can never repay
But service is rendered in love
And leads to a brighter day.

We will be vexed in spirit
With no power from God above
If we attempt to do from duty
What can only be done in love.

Do this; do that
Do what is required
It might make us feel holy
But it's not what God desired.

You see, God declared,
I'll give them a new start
I'll move my law from their heads
And I'll put it in their hearts.

So God sent Jesus
To pay-off our debt of sin
To free us from the *Law of Duty*
And usher the *Law of Love* in.

So when we see that rugged cross
And view that empty tomb
We can shout, "Yes, duty killed Him,
But for love His life resumed!"

Jesus made it so good,
My sister and my brother,
The scripture now tells us
Just to love one another.

And when service is traded for duty
The scripture says again
There's no need for others to teach us
When the Spirit of Love moves in.

So when what you do for others
Begins to cut like a knife
Remember--duty kills
But Love gives life.

THE TRUTH
❈ ❈ ❈ ❈

You have to accept
God's Word is true
Even when that Word
Lands heavy on you.

Without God's perfect standard
There's nothing left
By which you can truly
Measure yourself.

And when we measure
We'll always come up short
We'll find every time
Our work is for naught.

Guess what?
God intended it that way
So we can finally see ourselves
And look up and say . . .

"Jesus, I've tried
But I have nothing left
I need You to save me
From my sin and myself."

And the angels will party
And the Dove will descend
And with outstretched arms
Jesus will welcome you in.

So don't mess with God's Word
Trying to make it fit you
Let every man be a liar
And God's Word be true.

When we admit the truth
That we're sinners . . . and sometimes jerks
Then the truth of God's Word
Can have its perfect work!

SHOUT WITH ME!
⌘⌘⌘⌘

Show me a miracle
People say
But I see miracles everyday
When bombs *don't* fall
And children play
Will anybody shout with me?

When you think about it
All the wrong we've done
And the sun still rose
After nine-one-one
And many repented and turned to God's Son
Will anybody shout with me?

When you treat me bad
From day to day
And I don't say what I used to say
And God lets me see
My enemies pay
Will anybody shout with me?

When you get the call
Heart pounding by the minute
Your daughter's car was totaled
But she wasn't in it
And she said, "Praise the Lord!"--and meant it
Will anybody shout with me?

When my friend lost his job the other day
They fired him on the spot
And blew him all away
But, now, he's got his dream job
And he *knows* God heard him pray
Will anybody shout with me?

Lord, we don't shout
Because of what You do
It's because You gave Your Word
And we *see* Your Word come true
You said, Weeping may endure for a night
And we *see* joy come in the morning light.

You said, Our trials come to make us strong
And we *see* ourselves grow as time moves along
You said, To call things as though they be
And then You do a *new* thing and let us see
Oh, Lord, You keep Your Word so faithfully
Will anybody shout with me?

And if you keep Your Word in things we can see
We know You'll keep your promise
For what is yet to be
And, yes, we can believe Jesus died to set us free
For Your Word declares it
And it stands eternally
Will anybody shout with me!!

PEAS IN THE POT
⌘⌘⌘⌘

I dreamed the other night
I made a pot of peas
Meaty, saucy, spicy--yum
No peas ever better than these.

I took my pot to a meeting
There was no food there
So it came as no surprise to me
When my peas became the fare.

The desire for my peas
I didn't exactly spurn
As long as I could share them
On my own terms.

They had to use clean spoons
Was the rule I made myself
Because I wanted to take home
All the peas that were left.

When I had to leave the room
And leave my peas alone
I hid my peas in the car
Rather than risk they'd be all gone.

The very next day
While driving down the street
I smelled a foul whiff
Coming out of the backseat.

Oh, no! Oh, no!
I lamented
I lost my yummy peas!
I repented.

I awoke from that dream
With a shout and a start
Blood racing, chest pounding
With a prayer on my heart.

Lord, I'm so sorry
Now, I see my lot
I didn't share my peas
And they spoiled in the pot!

I felt like that servant
Burying his talent given
Instead of meeting the needs
In the lives of the living.

You gave me Your best, Lord
For others to enjoy
But I hoarded it for myself
Not believing You'd give me more.

There's no doubt; You'll give me more
Peas even better than the ones before
But I'll never know until I let go
Release them and watch You make them soar.

So from now on, Lord
I promise; I do
To freely share the blessings
I get from you.

And then later that day
The stock market dropped--humph
If you don't share your peas
They spoil in the pot.

BLIND SPOTS
⌘⌘⌘⌘

How in the world
Can we ever begin to fix
Our own blind spots?

By their very nature
It means we cannot see
What looks horrible to you
Pssh . . . may look fine to me.

That's why God is the Righteous Judge
And Jesus our Peacemaker
Because only The Holy Spirit
Is able to change our nature.

The same grace it takes to save us
Is the same grace it takes to grow us
For only the Lord Jesus
Can ever truly know us.

For no matter how we try
Good intentions--do or die
It's impossible for us to see
Around our own blind spots.

So trust Jesus to save you
Trust Jesus to grow you
He has never lost a case.

And then give Him the praise
Throughout all your days
For His unmerited,
Amazing grace!

'BENZES
⌘⌘⌘⌘

'Benzes valet parked
In front of the cancer ward
Close to the end
You want to talk to God.

Tell Him who you are
And the things you've done
But He only wants to know,
"What did you do with my Son?"

His Only Begotten
Sent from heaven's gates
To pay the heavy price
For every sin that we would make.

Symbols of distinction
Fading in the gloom
The only one that matters
Is Christ's empty tomb.

Unless you put your faith
In the righteousness He lends
It's not going to matter
That you drove a 'Benz.

Rockin'
⌘⌘⌘⌘

Old folk sitting on the front porch
Rockin'

Thinking 'bout the past
Things that made them laugh
In a present
That is far too serious

People that they knew
Things the Lord
Brought them through
Just enjoying the view

Ignoring the future, too
Rockin'

About the Author
Jeanetta Britt

Award-winning author, Jeanetta Britt, began writing in Dallas, Texas, but has recently returned to her native Alabama. She is a Fisk University graduate with a master's degree from The University of Michigan.

Miss Britt writes fiction novels filled with drama and suspense, which excite the senses and inspire the soul. "While being swept up in the story," she says, "I want my readers to *feel* the love of Jesus and find redemption in Him, like I did." She also writes inspirational poetry.

Her compelling novel series includes: ***Pickin' Ground*** (ISBN 0-9712363-3-x); ***In Due Season*** (ISBN 0-9712363-4-8); and ***Lottie*** (ISBN 0-9712363-6-4). In *Pickin' Ground*, Lottie and her boss, Raymond, run from a masked murderer on their way to making some life-transforming choices. In, *In Due Season*, Lottie returns home to rural Alabama to help her mother and her community, only to find her own true purpose and true love. In, *Lottie*, she becomes the first female African-American senator in Alabama, gets married, and the good-ole-boys are trying to kill her. Her priorities are out of whack, but through faith and prayer she comes to realize, "There's no love like married love!"

Empty Envelope (ISBN 978-0-9712363-5-6) is a story of love deferred by severe trials and personal sacrifice until the Lord brings it forth in great triumph. "Yes, we *can* do it God's way and win!"

In ***W.O.O.F.*** (ISBN 978-0-9712363-8-7), the Women of Overcoming Faith put *'one another'* love to the test.

In addition to ***Flittin' & Flyin'*** (ISBN 978-0-9712363-9-4), her poetry offerings include: ***Under the Influence--Spoken Praise*** (ISBN 0-9712363-7-2); ***Poems from the Fast*** (ISBN 0-9712363-0-5); ***Reunion*** (ISBN 0-9712363-1-3); and ***Third Ear*** (ISBN 0-9712363-2-1).

www.ingramcontent.com/pod-product-compliance
Lightning Source LLC
Chambersburg PA
CBHW060426050426
42449CB00009B/2158